For all the girls & boys that keep asking How & Why

"Don't be afraid of hard work. Nothing worthwhile comes easily.
Don't let others discourage you or tell you that you can't do it. In my day,
I was told women didn't go into chemistry. I saw no reason why we couldn't."
-Gertrude B. Elion, 1988 Nobel Prize in Medicine

With special thanks to **Olivia Wong, Monita Sen, Lewis Scott, Torrin Nuttall, and Jessica Lee.**

All rights reserved.
The authorship and copyright rights belong to Kameel Vohra in accordance to the Copyright Act, Singapore.
No part of this publication may be reproduced, stored in a retrieval system, or transmitted in any form or by
any means, electronic, mechanical, photocopying, recording or otherwise, without prior permission of the author.
A record of this book is available from the Singapore National Library.
First published in 2020. Story & text by Kameel Vohra. Illustrations by Alvin Adhi Mulyono.
Edited by Crystal Watanabe of Pikko's House.

ISBN 978-981-14-8549-7 (eBook) ISBN 978-981-14-8548-0 (Paperback) ISBN 978-981-14-8547-3 (Hardcover)

Visit our website at: **www.anikabooks.com**

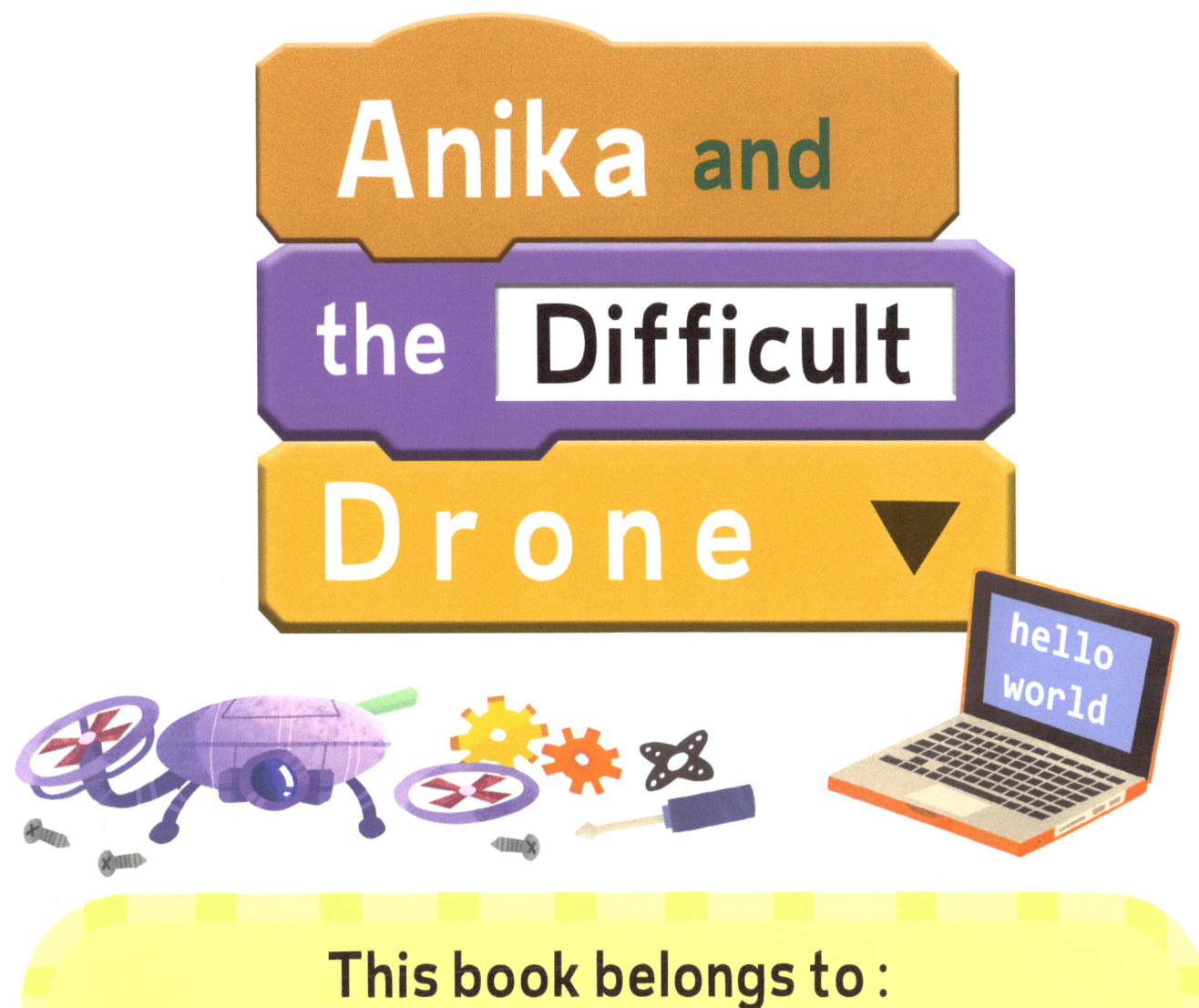

Anika and the Difficult Drone

This book belongs to :

....

Oh no! Anika is stuck.
She's building a new drone.
"I need some help," she declared.
"I can't do this alone."

"I know! I'll ask Grandma. She'll help it soar." But Grandma says, "Shhhhh!" and shuts her door.

"That's okay. I'll ask my brother. He'll explain the instructions."
But he's busy doing his homework, reading about deductions.

"Who else? I'll ask my mum. She's bound to be free!"
But Mum is helping sick patients. Anika sighs. "No time to help me!"

"Wait, I'll ask my dad!
He'll know what to do."
But Dad's on the phone,
He waves and says "I'm sure you'll make it through."

"It's just not fair!" she cried.
"I need help, and everyone's here.
But no one wants to help me.
They just say things like 'Not now, dear.'"

Anika feels angry and upset.
She really wants to play with her drone.
She's determined to finish it.
Even if she has to do it alone!

Anika is trying really hard.
She wipes away a tear.
The door creaks, and as she looks up,
guess who should appear?

Dad's phone calls are over,
He says, "Anika don't cry.
Let's finish this drone,
then we can take it out to fly."

Mum's last patient has left.
After a few big hugs,
she says, "Don't worry, darling.
Together, we will fix all the bugs."

Homework done, here comes her brother to move all his things.
He says, "You need some space for your drone to spread its wings."

Grandma has finished her game and brings,
milk and biscuits on a tray,
She says, "Have a quick snack,
and then we can all play!"

Anika didn't need to cry.
Her family loves her big smile.
Sometimes all you need to do
is stay focused and wait a little while!

Look at these pictures from the story, do you know which order they should be in?

 **How much do you remember from the story? Let's find out:**

Remembering
- Who are the main characters?
- How many trophy cup's can you find?
- What job does Anika's mum do?
- Where does her dad work?

Understanding
- Which part of the story did you like best? Why?
- What made Anika unhappy/upset?
- Once she calmed down, what did she decide to do?
- Who helped her? When did they come?

Applying
- What could Anika have done differently?
- What is the moral of the story?
- What hard things have you done on your own?
- Write down difficult things that you really want to do (or learn)

Visit our website for lots of exciting coloring sheets, puzzles and activities!

anikabooks.com/activities

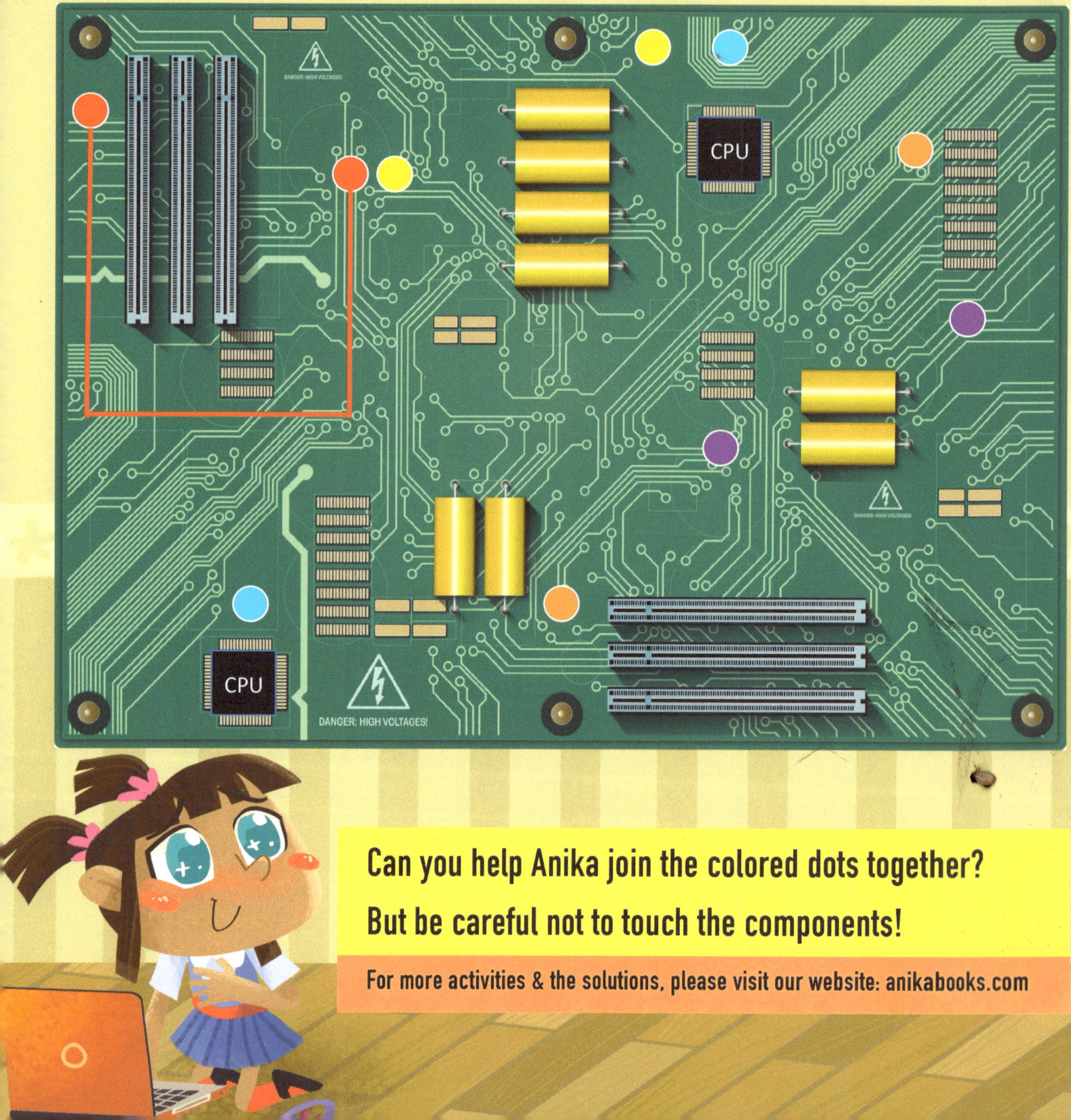

Can you help Anika join the colored dots together?

But be careful not to touch the components!

For more activities & the solutions, please visit our website: anikabooks.com

Authors Note

I've tried to pack lots of meaning into a small single story,
so that re-reading it offers different lessons each time.
Which made this a really fun (but challenging) book to put together.

In this story I hope to show girls & boys that there are exciting
science/engineering projects they can do, that mums can code,
dads often work from home, many families have mixed ethnicities,
that your parents love you even when they're busy -
and to have patience & perseverance. Phew!

I hope your kids and you enjoyed reading the story!
Please leave a review on Amazon (search Anika and the Difficult Drone).
I would be forever grateful.

With thanks,

Kameel

Please leave a review

http://anikabooks.com/difficult-drone-review/

CPSIA information can be obtained
at www.ICGtesting.com
Printed in the USA
LVHW071231070323
741092LV00012B/664